THE LIFE CYCLE OF A

Dog

By Colleen Sexton

BELLWETHER MEDIA • MINNEAPOLIS, MN

Note to Librarians, Teachers, and Parents:

Blastoff! Readers are carefully developed by literacy experts and combine standards-based content with developmentally appropriate text.

Level 1 provides the most support through repetition of high-frequency words, light text, predictable sentence patterns, and strong visual support.

Level 2 offers early readers a bit more challenge through varied simple sentences, increased text load, and less repetition of high-frequency words.

Level 3 advances early-fluent readers toward fluency through increased text and concept load, less reliance on visuals, longer sentences, and more literary language.

Level 4 builds reading stamina by providing more text per page, increased use of punctuation, greater variation in sentence patterns, and increasingly challenging vocabulary.

Level 5 encourages children to move from "learning to read" to "reading to learn" by providing even more text, varied writing styles, and less familiar topics.

Whichever book is right for your reader, Blastoff! Readers are the perfect books to build confidence and encourage a love of reading that will last a lifetime!

This edition first published in 2010 by Bellwether Media, Inc.

Library of Congress Cataloging-in-Publication Data
Sexton, Colleen A., 1967–
  The life cycle of a dog / by Colleen Sexton.
    p. cm. — (Blastoff! Readers life cycles)
  Includes bibliographical references and index.
  Summary: "Developed by literacy experts for students in kindergarten through grade three, this book follows dogs as they transform from puppies to adults. Through leveled text and related images, young readers will watch these creatures grow through every stage of life"–Provided by publisher.
  ISBN 978-1-60014-307-6 (hardcover : alk. paper)
  1. Dogs–Life cycles–Juvenile literature. I. Title.
QL737.C22S49 2010
636.7–dc22
                          2009037262

Printed in the United States of America, North Mankato, MN.
010110   1149

Contents

Dogs are **mammals**. They are popular pets. They have lived with people for more than 10,000 years!

There are around 400 **breeds** of dogs. This breed of dog is called a Dalmatian.

All dogs grow and change in stages. The stages of a dog's **life cycle** are birth, puppy, and adult.

adult

birth

puppy

A female dog gives birth to a puppy.
A puppy is part of a **litter**. There are
many brothers and sisters in a litter!

The puppy's fur is wet.
The mother licks the
puppy clean and it
starts to breathe.

The puppy cannot hear or open its eyes.
It can smell and feel. The puppy uses
these senses to stay close to its mother.

The puppy crawls to its mother's belly. It is ready to eat. The puppy drinks milk from its mother.

The puppy sleeps for 20 hours a day.
Sleeping helps the puppy grow.

The puppy's eyes open and it can hear.
The puppy starts to explore and play.
It can wag its tail and bark.

The puppy's legs become stronger. It can walk and run when it is four weeks old.

At six weeks old the puppy has teeth. It eats
solid food instead of its mother's milk.

The puppy is ready to leave its mother when it is eight weeks old. The puppy goes to a new home.

The puppy eats more and is full of energy.
It grows quickly.

The puppy is six months old. It has grown
tall. It has strong adult teeth.

The puppy is fully grown
when it is about one year
old. It is now an adult.

Adult dogs can have puppies. A male dog and a female dog **mate**.

Puppies grow inside the female dog for nine weeks. Her belly grows larger.

The female gives birth to a litter. These tiny puppies are the beginning of a new life cycle!

Glossary

breed—a group of animals that have the same body features; the most popular dog breeds are Labrador Retriever, Yorkshire Terrier, German Shepherd, Golden Retriever, and Beagle.

life cycle—the stages of life of an animal; a life cycle includes being born, growing up, having young, and dying.

litter—a group of animals born at the same time to one mother; the size of a dog litter depends on the kind of dog; most litters have between one and ten puppies.

mammal—a warm-blooded animal with a backbone; most mammals have hair on their bodies; female mammals make milk to feed their young.

mate—to join together to produce young

To Learn More

AT THE LIBRARY
Kalman, Bobbie. *What Is a Life Cycle?* New York, N.Y.: Crabtree Publishing, 1998.

Magloff, Lisa. *Puppy*. New York, N.Y.: DK Publishing, 2005.

Royston, Angela. *Life Cycle of a Dog*. Chicago, Ill.: Heinemann Library, 2000.

ON THE WEB
Learning more about life cycles is as easy as 1, 2, 3.

1. Go to www.factsurfer.com.

2. Enter "life cycles" into the search box.

3. Click the "Surf" button and you will see a list of related Web sites.

With factsurfer.com, finding more information is just a click away.

Index

The images in this book are reproduced through the courtesy of: Juniors Bildarchiv, front cover (adult, puppy), pp. 6 (adult, puppy)7, 10, 12, 13, 21; Kathleen Campell, front cover (birth), pp. 6 (birth), 8; blickwinkel / Alamy, front cover (young adult), p. 17; Snapdesign / Dreamstime.com, p. 4; Bill Losh, p. 5; Sabine Stuewer/Kimballstock, pp. 9, 19; Lynn M. Stone/Kimballstock, p. 11; tbkmedia.de / Alamy, p. 14; T. Ozonas, p. 15; Alexander Raths, p. 16; Ron Kimball/Kimballstock, p. 18; John Daniels, p. 20.